PRINCEWILL LAGANG

The Road to Happily Ever After: Christian Marriage Wisdom

First published by PRINCEWILL LAGANG 2023

Copyright © 2023 by Princewill Lagang

All rights reserved. No part of this publication may be reproduced, stored or transmitted in any form or by any means, electronic, mechanical, photocopying, recording, scanning, or otherwise without written permission from the publisher. It is illegal to copy this book, post it to a website, or distribute it by any other means without permission.

Princewill Lagang asserts the moral right to be identified as the author of this work.

First edition

This book was professionally typeset on Reedsy. Find out more at reedsy.com

Contents

1	Foundations of a Christ-Centered Marriage	1
2	The Covenant of Communication	4
3	Building Trust and Security	7
4	Nurturing Intimacy and Emotional Connection	10
5	Fostering Growth and Individuality	13
6	Stewardship of Finances and Resources	16
7	Navigating Life's Challenges Together	19
8	Building a Lasting Legacy	22
9	Cultivating a Heart of Gratitude and Worship	25
10	Embracing the Journey	28
11	Cherishing the Present and Looking to the Future	31
12	A Lifetime of Love and Commitment	34

1

Foundations of a Christ-Centered Marriage

Introduction

In a world where the concept of marriage is continually evolving, Christian couples find solace and guidance in the unwavering principles of faith and love. The journey of building a Christ-centered marriage is akin to laying a strong foundation for a sturdy and enduring house. This chapter embarks on that journey, exploring the fundamental principles that underpin the beautiful institution of Christian marriage.

The Divine Blueprint

Before we delve into the practical aspects of a Christian marriage, it is essential to understand the divine blueprint laid out in the Bible. In Genesis 2:24, we find these profound words: "Therefore a man shall leave his father and his mother and hold fast to his wife, and they shall become one flesh." This verse sets the tone for the Christian understanding of marriage. It emphasizes leaving, cleaving, and becoming one, three cornerstones of a Christ-centered union.

1. Leaving: The act of leaving behind one's parents symbolizes the independence and autonomy that a couple must establish. It's not about neglecting or dishonoring parents but about the husband and wife forming a new family unit with its own unique identity and priorities.

2. Cleaving: To "hold fast" or "cleave" signifies the bond, the commitment, and the loyalty that a husband and wife must have towards one another. It's a covenant, not just a contract, where they promise to stay united through thick and thin.

3. Becoming One Flesh: The spiritual and physical oneness of marriage reflects the intimate connection that God designed for couples. It's about more than just physical intimacy; it's a profound unity of heart, mind, and soul.

God's Role in Marriage

Understanding the divine role in your marriage is crucial. God's presence in your relationship is like a third strand in a cord that cannot easily be broken (Ecclesiastes 4:12). Your faith is not a mere aspect of your life but a central pillar of your marriage. It is God who binds you together, supports you, and guides you on your journey.

Love, the Core of Marriage

At the heart of every successful Christian marriage is love. This is not just any love, but agape love, the selfless, sacrificial, and unconditional love that God has for us. In 1 Corinthians 13, often referred to as the "Love Chapter," the Apostle Paul beautifully describes the attributes of agape love. This kind of love is patient, kind, not envious or boastful, not self-seeking, and it never fails. It is the love that should flow between spouses.

Marriage as a Reflection of Christ and the Church

Ephesians 5:25-27 provides a profound insight into the Christian marriage model. It states, "Husbands, love your wives, just as Christ loved the church and gave himself up for her." This verse underscores the sacrificial love husbands are called to demonstrate, mirroring Christ's love for His Church. Wives, on the other hand, are called to submit to their husbands as the Church submits to Christ. The marriage relationship is meant to reflect the profound love and submission between Christ and His Church.

Conclusion

As you embark on the journey of building a Christ-centered marriage, remember that it begins with a strong foundation rooted in biblical principles. Leave, cleave, and become one flesh, embracing God's role and agape love as the core of your relationship. Your marriage is a reflection of Christ and the Church, a sacred union designed to honor God and bring joy and fulfillment to your lives. In the chapters ahead, we will explore the practical aspects of living out these principles and achieving your happily ever after.

2

The Covenant of Communication

Introduction

Communication is the lifeblood of any successful marriage. In this chapter, we will explore the significance of effective communication in the context of Christian marriage. Just as God communicates with His people, husbands and wives must communicate openly and honestly with one another to build a strong and lasting union.

The Power of Words

Proverbs 18:21 reminds us that "death and life are in the power of the tongue." Words have the ability to heal or wound, uplift or tear down. In your marriage, the words you choose are critical. You can either speak life into your relationship or bring about its slow demise.

1. Edifying Words: Ephesians 4:29 encourages us to speak only words that build others up. In your marriage, this means using words that express love, appreciation, and encouragement. Compliment your spouse's strengths, support their endeavors, and express gratitude for their presence in your life.

2. Effective Listening: Communication is a two-way street. It's not just about speaking but also about listening attentively to your spouse. James 1:19 advises, "Let every person be quick to hear, slow to speak, slow to anger." This principle is essential in resolving conflicts and truly understanding each other's needs.

Conflict Resolution

Conflict is a natural part of any relationship, but how it's handled can make or break a marriage. The Bible provides guidance on resolving conflicts in Matthew 18:15-17, teaching us to address issues directly and seek reconciliation.

1. Speak the Truth in Love: Ephesians 4:15 emphasizes speaking the truth in love. When conflicts arise, share your concerns honestly but with a spirit of love and respect. Avoid harsh words or contemptuous attitudes.

2. Forgiveness and Reconciliation: Colossians 3:13 advises, "Bear with each other and forgive one another if any of you has a grievance against someone. Forgive as the Lord forgave you." This reflects the importance of forgiveness and the healing power it holds in a marriage.

Prayer and Seeking God's Guidance

Prayer is an essential component of Christian marriage. It is a means of seeking God's guidance, wisdom, and strength in your journey together. James 5:16 reminds us of the power of prayer: "The prayer of a righteous person is powerful and effective."

1. Praying Together: Praying together as a couple not only strengthens your connection with God but also deepens your emotional intimacy. Sharing your hopes, fears, and dreams with God and each other fosters a unique bond.

2. Seeking God's Will: In your communication, seek God's guidance. His wisdom can help you make important decisions, handle challenges, and align your marriage with His divine purpose.

Conclusion

Effective communication is the cornerstone of a thriving Christian marriage. Choose your words carefully, practice active listening, and employ biblical principles in conflict resolution. Incorporate prayer into your daily lives, individually and together, as it strengthens your connection with each other and with God. In the subsequent chapters, we will explore further facets of a Christ-centered marriage, all of which hinge on the strong foundation of open and loving communication.

3

Building Trust and Security

Introduction

Trust is the bedrock of a strong and enduring Christian marriage. Without trust, the relationship is like a house built on shifting sand. In this chapter, we will delve into the importance of trust, how to nurture it, and the sense of security it brings to your journey on the road to happily ever after.

The Foundation of Trust

Trust begins with a promise, and the most fundamental promise in marriage is the marriage covenant itself. When you exchanged vows, you made a commitment to love, honor, and cherish one another. Trust is the belief that your spouse will honor these vows and remain faithful to them.

Transparency and Honesty

Open and honest communication is the first step in building trust. Proverbs 12:22 tells us, "Lying lips are an abomination to the Lord, but those who act faithfully are his delight." When you are transparent with your spouse, you create an environment of faithfulness and truth.

1. Full Disclosure: Transparency means sharing your thoughts, feelings, and actions with your spouse. This doesn't mean every detail of your life must be an open book, but important matters should be discussed openly.

2. Confession and Forgiveness: When mistakes are made, as they inevitably will be, a Christian marriage is marked by the willingness to confess and seek forgiveness. 1 John 1:9 reminds us that "If we confess our sins, he is faithful and just to forgive us our sins and to cleanse us from all unrighteousness."

Protecting Your Marriage

Just as you trust your spouse, you must also protect your marriage. This includes guarding your relationship from influences that could undermine trust. Proverbs 4:23 advises, "Above all else, guard your heart, for everything you do flows from it."

1. Fidelity: Faithfulness in marriage is not just about sexual fidelity but also emotional fidelity. It means staying committed to your spouse and not allowing outside influences to interfere with your bond.

2. Healthy Boundaries: Setting healthy boundaries with individuals outside your marriage, such as friends or coworkers, can protect your relationship from potential pitfalls.

Rebuilding Trust

Sometimes, trust can be broken. In such cases, it's essential to know that it's possible to rebuild trust through mutual effort and with God's help. Romans 15:7 encourages us to "Accept one another, then, just as Christ accepted you, in order to bring praise to God."

1. Repentance and Forgiveness: The process of rebuilding trust often involves repentance for the one who broke it and forgiveness from the one who was hurt. This can be a challenging but transformative experience.

2. Counsel and Support: Seeking the guidance of a pastor or Christian counselor can be instrumental in the healing process.

Conclusion

Trust and security are intertwined in a Christian marriage. Trust is a precious gift that you both give and receive, and it's built on transparency, honesty, and the faithfulness to your marriage vows. Protecting your marriage from threats and understanding the process of rebuilding trust are important aspects of nurturing this vital aspect of your relationship. In the following chapters, we will explore additional elements that contribute to your road to happily ever after in a Christ-centered marriage.

4

Nurturing Intimacy and Emotional Connection

Introduction

In a Christian marriage, true intimacy goes far beyond physical closeness. It extends to a deep emotional connection that binds husband and wife as one. In this chapter, we will explore the various dimensions of intimacy, from the emotional to the physical, and how they contribute to your journey on the road to happily ever after.

Emotional Intimacy

Emotional intimacy is the foundation of a Christ-centered marriage. It involves sharing your innermost thoughts, feelings, and vulnerabilities with your spouse, creating a safe and nurturing space for one another.

1. Active Listening: One of the primary ways to build emotional intimacy is through active listening. This means giving your spouse your full attention, expressing empathy, and validating their feelings.

2. Vulnerability: Sharing your fears, hopes, and dreams with your spouse fosters emotional closeness. Ephesians 4:32 advises us to "Be kind to one another, tenderhearted, forgiving one another, as God in Christ forgave you."

Spiritual Intimacy

In a Christian marriage, your spiritual connection is also a crucial dimension of intimacy. Your shared faith can deepen your bond in profound ways.

1. Praying Together: As mentioned in Chapter 2, praying together as a couple is an intimate practice that strengthens your spiritual connection. It's a way of inviting God into your relationship.

2. Worship and Scripture: Attending church, studying the Bible, or participating in spiritual activities together can help you grow closer to each other and to God.

Physical Intimacy

Physical intimacy is a beautiful and sacred part of marriage. In 1 Corinthians 7:3-4, it is written, "The husband should fulfill his marital duty to his wife, and likewise the wife to her husband. The wife does not have authority over her own body but yields it to her husband." Physical intimacy, when expressed within the bounds of marriage, is a reflection of the unity and love between husband and wife.

1. Nurturing Romance: Keep the romance alive by dating your spouse, surprising each other with acts of love, and being attentive to each other's physical and emotional needs.

2. Communication: Open communication about your desires and boundaries is essential. Respect each other's needs and preferences in this area.

Challenges in Nurturing Intimacy

There may be challenges along the way in nurturing intimacy, such as past wounds, stress, or miscommunication. However, with patience and God's guidance, you can overcome these obstacles.

1. Forgiveness and Healing: Addressing past wounds and seeking forgiveness for any hurts or misunderstandings is an essential step in moving forward.

2. Seeking Guidance: If intimacy challenges persist, don't hesitate to seek guidance from a counselor or a trusted pastor who can offer support and strategies for rekindling intimacy.

Conclusion

Nurturing emotional, spiritual, and physical intimacy in your Christian marriage is a lifelong journey. It's about continually deepening your connection with your spouse and with God. These aspects of intimacy not only strengthen your relationship but also contribute to your journey on the road to a happy and fulfilling Christ-centered marriage. In the upcoming chapters, we will explore more aspects of building a successful and God-honoring marriage.

5

Fostering Growth and Individuality

Introduction

In a Christian marriage, the path to happily ever after is not about losing your individuality but rather about fostering personal growth while nurturing the growth of your relationship. In this chapter, we will explore how to strike a balance between personal development and the unity of marriage, finding a harmonious blend that leads to a thriving Christ-centered union.

Embracing Individuality

Before you are a couple, you are individuals with unique qualities, interests, and dreams. God created each of you with a purpose and a distinct identity. It is vital to honor and nurture your individuality even as you build a life together.

Balancing Independence and Togetherness

1. Personal Growth: Proverbs 4:7 tells us, "The beginning of wisdom is

this: Get wisdom, and whatever you get, get insight." Encourage each other's personal growth and the pursuit of individual goals, whether they be educational, career-oriented, or personal passions. Support each other in becoming the best version of yourselves.

2. Interests and Hobbies: Pursuing separate interests and hobbies can be healthy for a marriage. It allows you to maintain your unique identities while providing opportunities to come together and share experiences.

Unity in Marriage

While it is essential to nurture individuality, maintaining a sense of unity is equally critical. Ephesians 4:3 reminds us to "make every effort to keep the unity of the Spirit through the bond of peace."

1. Shared Values: Revisit your shared values and beliefs regularly. Understanding what you both stand for helps to solidify your bond.

2. Communication: Regularly communicate your dreams, plans, and goals with each other. This ensures that you are on the same page and can work together toward common objectives.

Supporting Each Other's Dreams

Your spouse's dreams and aspirations should be as important to you as your own. Philippians 2:4 advises us to "not only look to your own interests but also to the interests of others."

1. Encouragement: Offer words of encouragement and support for your spouse's dreams. Celebrate their achievements and help them through challenges.

2. Prayer: Include your spouse's dreams and aspirations in your prayers.

Praying together for each other's success can create a strong sense of partnership.

Overcoming Challenges

There may be times when the pursuit of personal growth and individuality in marriage encounters obstacles. It's crucial to address these challenges together.

1. Balancing Priorities: As your family grows, you may need to reassess and balance priorities. Discuss your goals and make necessary adjustments to ensure harmony in your family life.

2. Respecting Boundaries: Respect each other's boundaries, and communicate openly about your individual needs and limitations.

Conclusion

A thriving Christian marriage is one in which individual growth is nurtured and supported within the context of a strong, unified relationship. Embrace your individuality and personal dreams while maintaining a sense of unity through shared values, open communication, and mutual support. As you journey on the road to happily ever after, this balance will be instrumental in creating a fulfilling and God-honoring marriage. In the upcoming chapters, we will continue to explore essential aspects of building a successful and enduring Christian marriage.

6

Stewardship of Finances and Resources

Introduction

The way a Christian couple manages their finances and resources can significantly impact their marriage. In this chapter, we will explore the principles of financial stewardship, providing guidance on how to handle money, plan for the future, and navigate financial challenges while keeping God at the center of your financial decisions.

Understanding Financial Stewardship

Financial stewardship is the practice of managing money and resources with wisdom, integrity, and a recognition that everything ultimately belongs to God. It involves using your financial blessings to fulfill God's purposes.

Shared Financial Goals

1. Establish Shared Goals: Sit down with your spouse to discuss your financial goals, both short-term and long-term. These goals should be aligned with your values and priorities as a Christian couple.

2. Budgeting: Create a budget that outlines your income, expenses, and savings. Proverbs 21:5 advises, "The plans of the diligent lead to profit as surely as haste leads to poverty."

Honest Communication

1. Transparency: Be open and honest about your financial situation. Share your income, expenses, and any debts. This transparency builds trust in your relationship.

2. Regular Financial Check-Ins: Schedule regular financial meetings with your spouse to assess your progress towards your financial goals, adjust your budget as needed, and ensure you are on the same page.

Financial Responsibility

1. Avoid Debt: Proverbs 22:7 reminds us, "The rich rule over the poor, and the borrower is slave to the lender." Strive to avoid unnecessary debt and manage existing debt responsibly.

2. Savings and Emergency Funds: Prioritize saving for emergencies, future expenses, and retirement. This is not just for your security but also to honor God by being good stewards of the resources He has entrusted to you.

Generosity and Giving

God calls us to be generous and give to those in need. Proverbs 11:25 says, "A generous person will prosper; whoever refreshes others will be refreshed."

1. Tithing: Consider tithing as a way to support your local church and the work of God's Kingdom. This act of giving reflects your trust in God's provision.

2. Charitable Giving: Additionally, allocate a portion of your income for charitable giving. Supporting charitable causes is a way to extend God's love and blessings to others.

Financial Challenges and Conflict Resolution

Financial challenges can put a strain on a marriage, but with the right approach, they can be opportunities for growth.

1. Seeking God's Guidance: Turn to God in prayer during financial difficulties, seeking His wisdom and provision.

2. Conflict Resolution: Approach financial conflicts with grace and respect. Remember that your ultimate goal is unity and alignment with God's plan for your marriage.

Conclusion

Financial stewardship in a Christian marriage involves working together to manage your resources wisely, in alignment with your values and faith. Embrace shared financial goals, open communication, and a commitment to financial responsibility. Give generously, seek God's guidance, and navigate financial challenges with grace. By keeping God at the center of your financial decisions, you can strengthen your marriage and fulfill His purpose for your life together. In the upcoming chapters, we will continue to explore the essential aspects of building a successful and enduring Christian marriage.

7

Navigating Life's Challenges Together

Introduction

Life is full of challenges, and in a Christian marriage, you'll undoubtedly face your share of difficulties. In this chapter, we will explore the importance of facing life's challenges together, drawing strength from your faith, your commitment to each other, and the support of your Christian community.

The Unpredictability of Life

Life's challenges come in various forms: health crises, financial setbacks, career changes, loss of loved ones, and personal struggles. While these difficulties can be daunting, they can also become opportunities for growth and strengthening your marriage.

Relying on Your Faith

1. Prayer and Spiritual Support: Turn to prayer and seek solace in your faith. In James 5:13, we are advised to pray when facing suffering. Seek support from your church or Christian community, as they can provide valuable spiritual and emotional support.

2. Trusting God's Plan: Understand that God has a plan for your life and your marriage. While it may not always be clear, trust that God is with you, guiding you through challenges.

Solidarity and Teamwork

1. Facing Challenges Together: Approach challenges as a team. Your marriage is a partnership, and you can tackle difficulties more effectively when you work together.

2. Open Communication: Maintain open communication with your spouse. Share your concerns, fears, and hopes. In times of difficulty, this connection is invaluable.

Resilience and Adaptability

1. Flexibility: Be open to adjusting your plans and expectations. Life's challenges may require you to pivot and adapt to new circumstances.

2. Learning and Growth: Challenges often bring opportunities for personal and relational growth. Embrace the lessons learned from adversity.

Seeking Professional Help

There may be times when the challenges you face require professional assistance.

1. Counseling: Consider seeking counseling or therapy to navigate complex issues. A Christian counselor can provide guidance that aligns with your faith.

2. Support Groups: Engage with support groups within your Christian community. Sharing experiences with others who have faced similar

challenges can offer comfort and guidance.

Strength in Unity

1. Ecclesiastes 4:9-10: This passage reminds us, "Two are better than one because they have a good return for their labor. If either of them falls down, one can help the other up." In your Christian marriage, you are each other's support system.

2. Serving Together: Consider serving others as a couple. Volunteering or assisting those in need can be a way to strengthen your bond and bring positivity into your lives.

Conclusion

In a Christian marriage, facing life's challenges together is a testament to the strength of your faith and the depth of your commitment to each other. Rely on your faith, communicate openly, and embrace challenges as opportunities for growth. Seek support from your Christian community and be willing to adapt and learn. Through unity and resilience, you can navigate life's challenges and continue on the road to happily ever after. In the following chapters, we will continue to explore the key aspects of building a successful and enduring Christian marriage.

8

Building a Lasting Legacy

Introduction

Your Christian marriage is not just about your life together; it's about the legacy you create for future generations. In this chapter, we will explore the importance of building a lasting legacy through your marriage, one that reflects your faith, values, and commitment to God.

Understanding Legacy

A legacy is the impact you leave behind, the values you pass down, and the influence you have on others. In a Christian marriage, your legacy extends beyond your lifetime.

Living Out Your Faith

1. Consistency: Living a life that consistently reflects your faith and values is essential. Your actions and choices are a testament to your belief in God.

2. Integrity: Integrity is the foundation of a strong legacy. Proverbs 20:7

reminds us, "The righteous lead blameless lives; blessed are their children after them." Your integrity will inspire and guide your children and others who look up to you.

Passing Down Values

1. Teaching and Discipleship: Share your faith with your children and grandchildren. Teach them the importance of following Christ and living out His teachings.

2. Service and Generosity: Instill values of service and generosity in your family. Model compassion and the importance of helping others.

Family Traditions

1. Spiritual Traditions: Create family traditions that center around your faith, such as regular family prayers, Bible readings, and acts of service to the community.

2. Celebrations: Celebrate Christian holidays and milestones in a way that honors your faith and brings your family together.

Marital Health and Unity

1. Strong Marital Relationship: A lasting legacy starts with a strong marriage. Your relationship serves as a model for your children and grandchildren. Continue to invest in your marriage and maintain a loving, supportive partnership.

2. Conflict Resolution: Show your family how to navigate challenges and conflicts in a Christ-like manner. Demonstrating forgiveness and reconciliation is a powerful lesson.

Passing Down Stories and Wisdom

1. Oral Traditions: Share family stories and the wisdom you've gained over the years. These stories can provide guidance and inspiration to the next generation.

2. Mentorship: Be open to mentorship within your family. Offer guidance and support to younger family members as they navigate their own paths.

Being an Example in Your Community

1. Community Involvement: Extend your legacy beyond your family by getting involved in your Christian community. Your actions can inspire others and leave a lasting impact.

2. Leadership: Consider taking on leadership roles within your church or other Christian organizations. Your leadership can help shape the faith and values of those you serve.

Conclusion

Building a lasting legacy through your Christian marriage is a noble and deeply meaningful endeavor. By consistently living out your faith, passing down values, creating family traditions, maintaining a strong marital relationship, and being an example in your community, you can inspire and guide future generations in their own faith journeys. As you continue your journey on the road to happily ever after, remember the profound impact you have on the world around you and the legacy you are building for the glory of God. In the upcoming chapters, we will explore additional facets of building a successful and enduring Christian marriage.

9

Cultivating a Heart of Gratitude and Worship

Introduction

Gratitude and worship are essential aspects of a thriving Christian marriage. In this chapter, we will explore the importance of cultivating a heart of gratitude and worship within your relationship, as it deepens your connection with God and with each other.

Gratitude as a Foundation

Gratitude is the foundation of a joyful and contented Christian marriage. It shifts the focus from what you lack to what you have, fostering an attitude of appreciation for the blessings in your life.

Counting Your Blessings

1. Daily Thankfulness: Begin and end each day with gratitude. Reflect on the blessings, no matter how small, and express thanks to God and to your

spouse.

2. Gratitude Journal: Consider keeping a gratitude journal where you record the things you are thankful for. Sharing this practice with your spouse can enhance your bond.

Fostering a Culture of Appreciation

1. Appreciation for Each Other: Regularly express appreciation to your spouse. Acknowledge their efforts, love, and support. Colossians 3:15 reminds us to "be thankful."

2. Compliments: Don't hesitate to offer sincere compliments to your spouse. These small gestures can uplift their spirits and strengthen your connection.

Worship in Daily Life

Worship is not confined to a church setting. It's about recognizing God's presence in your everyday life and expressing your love and devotion to Him.

Personal Worship

1. Prayer and Reflection: Dedicate time for personal prayer and reflection. It's a moment for you to connect with God, seek His guidance, and express your love for Him.

2. Bible Study: Engage in regular Bible study to deepen your understanding of God's Word. It can be a source of inspiration and wisdom in your marriage.

Worship as a Couple

1. Praying Together: Praying together as a couple deepens your spiritual connection. It's an act of surrender and unity, where you bring your joys,

worries, and gratitude before God.

2. Worship Music: Incorporate worship music into your daily life. Singing and listening to worship songs can create a sacred atmosphere in your home.

Serving Together

Service is a form of worship. When you serve others, you express your gratitude for the blessings in your life by being a blessing to those in need.

1. Volunteer as a Couple: Find opportunities to serve your community or church together. This shared experience can strengthen your bond and give your marriage a sense of purpose.

2. Acts of Kindness: Practice random acts of kindness toward each other and those around you. It's a way to express your love and gratitude through actions.

Conclusion

Cultivating a heart of gratitude and worship in your Christian marriage is a transformative practice. Gratitude reminds you of the blessings you share, fostering contentment and joy. Worship, both individually and as a couple, deepens your connection with God and with each other. By expressing appreciation, seeking God's presence in your daily life, and serving those in need, you can nurture a relationship filled with love, faith, and joy. As you continue your journey on the road to happily ever after, remember the profound impact of gratitude and worship in strengthening your Christian marriage. In the subsequent chapters, we will continue to explore essential aspects of building a successful and enduring relationship.

10

Embracing the Journey

Introduction

As you near the culmination of this book, it is important to reflect on the journey you've embarked upon in your Christian marriage. This chapter delves into the significance of embracing the journey, acknowledging the ups and downs, and remaining steadfast in your commitment to a God-honoring and fulfilling union.

Reflecting on the Path Traveled

Taking a moment to reflect on your journey so far can provide insight and perspective on how far you've come and where you are headed.

Gratitude for the Past: Take time to express gratitude for the experiences and lessons learned during your marriage. Remember the moments that have shaped your relationship.

Recognizing Growth: Acknowledge the growth you've experienced as individuals and as a couple. Consider how your faith and love have deepened over time.

Challenges Faced: Reflect on the challenges you've overcome together. Recognize the strength of your commitment and your ability to navigate difficult times.

Nurturing Your Connection with God

Your journey in a Christian marriage is deeply rooted in your relationship with God. To continue growing, nurture your connection with the Divine.

Personal Spiritual Growth: Seek ongoing spiritual growth as individuals. Consider what you can do to deepen your faith and reliance on God.

Couples' Spiritual Growth: Explore ways to grow spiritually as a couple. This might involve setting spiritual goals, attending faith-based retreats, or studying the Bible together.

Renewing Commitment

As your journey continues, take time to renew your commitment to each other and to God.

Vows Renewal: Consider renewing your marriage vows as a symbol of your ongoing commitment to your covenant.

Setting New Goals: Set new goals and aspirations for your marriage. What do you hope to achieve in the years to come? How do you envision your journey progressing?

Maintaining Connection

Connection is the lifeblood of your marriage. It's essential to maintain and strengthen the bond that sustains your relationship.

Quality Time: Make an effort to spend quality time together. Carve out moments for deep conversations, romantic getaways, and shared experiences.

Communication: Continue practicing open and honest communication. Regularly discuss your dreams, fears, and aspirations. This keeps you connected on a profound level.

Serving Together

Serving others as a couple can be a powerful way to strengthen your bond and make a positive impact on the world.

Acts of Kindness: Consistently practice acts of kindness and love towards each other. Small gestures of love can have a big impact.

Outreach: Extend your service to the community and the world. Find opportunities to give back and make a difference together.

Conclusion

Embracing the journey in your Christian marriage is about acknowledging the path you've traveled, nurturing your connection with God, renewing your commitment, and maintaining your connection with each other. Your journey is a testimony to the enduring love and faith that can thrive within a Christ-centered union. As you move forward on the road to happily ever after, remember that your commitment to God and to each other is a source of strength and purpose that will continue to guide you in building a successful and enduring Christian marriage.

11

Cherishing the Present and Looking to the Future

Introduction

In the final chapter of this book, we'll explore the importance of cherishing the present moment in your Christian marriage while also looking to the future with hope and purpose. Your journey to happily ever after is ongoing, and this chapter will guide you in embracing the fullness of your relationship.

Living in the Present

Living in the present is a gift that allows you to fully experience the joys and challenges of your marriage. It's about appreciating the here and now.

Mindfulness: Practice mindfulness by staying fully engaged in the moment. Let go of past regrets and future worries to savor the present.

Gratitude: Continue to cultivate gratitude for the blessings in your life.

Express thanks to God for the love and joy in your marriage.

Celebrating Milestones

Reflect on the milestones you've reached in your marriage. Celebrate these moments with joy and appreciation for the journey you've undertaken.

Anniversaries: Celebrate your marriage anniversaries in a meaningful way. Use these occasions to reminisce about your journey and express your love for each other.

Family Growth: If you have children, mark their milestones with love and support. As your family grows, cherish each moment of their development.

Looking to the Future

While cherishing the present, it's also essential to look to the future with hope and purpose. What you envision for your future can shape your actions in the present.

Setting New Goals: Reflect on your shared goals and aspirations. Set new goals and a vision for your marriage that align with your values and faith.

Continuing Growth: Commit to ongoing personal and relational growth. Seek opportunities for learning and development in your Christian marriage.

Passing Down Wisdom

As your journey continues, consider how you can pass down the wisdom you've gained to the next generation.

Mentorship: Offer mentorship and guidance to younger couples, sharing your experiences and the principles that have guided your marriage.

Legacy: Continue building a lasting legacy of faith and love that your children and grandchildren can carry forward in their own lives.

Maintaining Connection

A strong connection is at the heart of your marriage. To keep it thriving, invest in your relationship daily.

Date Nights: Continue to prioritize date nights and quality time with your spouse. Reconnect and nurture your emotional intimacy.

Communication: Keep communication open and honest. Discuss your dreams, challenges, and plans for the future regularly.

Conclusion

Cherishing the present and looking to the future is a balance that sustains your Christian marriage. By living in the present with mindfulness, gratitude, and celebration, you can fully appreciate the journey you're on. Simultaneously, setting new goals, passing down wisdom, and maintaining a strong connection will empower your future together. As you move forward on the road to happily ever after, remember that your Christian marriage is a beautiful and ongoing testament to your love, faith, and commitment to each other and to God.

12

A Lifetime of Love and Commitment

Introduction

This final chapter encapsulates the essence of a Christian marriage, focusing on the lifelong journey of love and commitment you've embarked upon. It celebrates the enduring nature of your relationship and provides guidance on how to keep the flame of love and faith burning brightly.

The Everlasting Nature of Christian Marriage

In Christian faith, marriage is not just a partnership but a sacred covenant. It is a lifelong commitment to love, honor, and cherish one another through all of life's seasons.

The Vow of Permanence: Reflect on the vows you exchanged on your wedding day. These vows embody the commitment to endure all challenges and joys together.

Renewal of Commitment: Consider renewing your marriage vows periodically as a way to reaffirm your commitment to each other and to God.

A LIFETIME OF LOVE AND COMMITMENT

Steadfast Love

Love is at the heart of your Christian marriage. It's a love that endures, perseveres, and remains steadfast in the face of adversity.

Agape Love: Agape love, a selfless and sacrificial love, is a model for your Christian marriage. It is the kind of love that God has for His children.

Forgiveness: The capacity to forgive and seek forgiveness is essential for enduring love. 1 Corinthians 13:4-7 reminds us that love is patient, kind, and keeps no record of wrongs.

Endurance Through Challenges

Christian marriages are not exempt from challenges, but they possess the strength to endure and overcome them.

Prayer and Faith: Turn to prayer and faith in times of hardship. Trust that God's guidance and support will see you through.

Seeking Help: Don't hesitate to seek help from trusted mentors, counselors, or clergy when facing significant challenges.

Intentional Partnership

To maintain a lifetime of love and commitment, your marriage must be an intentional partnership.

Continued Growth: Commit to ongoing personal and relational growth. Seek opportunities for learning and development as individuals and as a couple.

Communication: Effective communication remains essential in addressing conflicts and maintaining emotional intimacy.

Legacy of Love and Faith

Your Christian marriage is a legacy of love and faith that extends beyond your lifetime.

Passing Down Wisdom: Share the wisdom you've gained with others, including your children and grandchildren, to guide them in their own relationships.

Serving Others: Continue to serve others, both within and outside your Christian community. Your love and acts of service are a testament to your faith.

Conclusion

A lifetime of love and commitment in a Christian marriage is a testament to the enduring love of God. As you reflect on the journey you've undertaken, remember the significance of your vows, the steadfastness of your love, and the enduring faith that binds you together. Your Christian marriage is not just a partnership; it is a lifelong commitment to love, honor, and cherish one another through all of life's seasons. In the grand narrative of your faith and love, your marriage is a remarkable chapter. May it be filled with the beauty and grace of God's enduring love, guiding you on the road to a lifetime of happiness together.

Book Summary: The Road to Happily Ever After: Christian Marriage Wisdom

The Road to Happily Ever After: Christian Marriage Wisdom is a profound and comprehensive guide to building a strong, enduring, and God-centered

Christian marriage. In this enlightening book, readers embark on a journey through twelve chapters, each providing valuable insights and practical advice for couples seeking to strengthen their bonds and deepen their faith.

The book opens with a foundational exploration of the principles that underpin a Christian marriage. It emphasizes the importance of faith, trust, and a commitment to shared values as the cornerstones of a strong marital partnership. The initial chapters guide couples in understanding the essence of Christian marriage and how to build their relationship on a solid spiritual foundation.

As the journey continues, the book delves into key aspects of a successful Christian marriage. Readers are guided through topics such as effective communication, conflict resolution, nurturing emotional intimacy, and the importance of shared prayer and worship. Throughout these chapters, the authors emphasize the need for open and honest communication as well as the power of prayer in strengthening the marital bond.

The book also addresses the practical dimensions of marriage, such as financial stewardship and managing resources, while maintaining a focus on godly principles. It encourages couples to approach their finances with wisdom, integrity, and the recognition that everything ultimately belongs to God. By sharing practical advice on budgeting, savings, and charitable giving, the book helps couples navigate financial challenges while honoring their faith.

Throughout the journey, the authors underscore the significance of cherishing the present and looking to the future with hope and purpose. They encourage couples to live in the moment, express gratitude, and celebrate milestones together. Simultaneously, the book advises setting new goals, passing down wisdom, and maintaining a strong connection in order to build a lasting legacy and ensure a thriving future together.

In the final chapters, the authors highlight the enduring nature of Christian marriage. They remind readers of the solemn vows exchanged on their wedding day and encourage periodic renewals to reaffirm their commitment to each other and to God. The book emphasizes the importance of steadfast love, forgiveness, and endurance through life's challenges, all while embracing the intentional partnership that keeps the flame of love burning brightly.

In conclusion, The Road to Happily Ever After: Christian Marriage Wisdom is a comprehensive and insightful guide that not only provides practical advice but also infuses every aspect of marriage with the wisdom and love of the Christian faith. It is a valuable resource for couples seeking to build a strong, enduring, and God-honoring marriage, as well as for those who wish to navigate the challenges of life with faith and love at the forefront of their journey.

www.ingramcontent.com/pod-product-compliance
Lightning Source LLC
LaVergne TN
LVHW010440070526
838199LV00066B/6099